Luvvies In Verse

From West End Winks to Broadway Belly Laughs

100 plays and musicals in haiku

Thespis Percival Pantomime
Titania Prima Prima-donna

COPYRIGHT © 2023 TPP LLP
ALL RIGHTS RESERVED.

NO PART OF THIS BOOK CAN BE REPRODUCED IN ANY FORM OR BY WRITTEN, ELECTRONIC OR MECHANICAL, INCLUDING PHOTOCOPYING, RECORDING, OR BY ANY INFORMATION RETRIEVAL SYSTEM WITHOUT WRITTEN PERMISSION IN WRITING BY THE AUTHOR.

PRINTED IN GREAT BRITAIN
ALTHOUGH EVERY PRECAUTION HAS BEEN TAKEN IN THE PREPARATION OF THIS BOOK, THE PUBLISHER AND AUTHOR ASSUME NO RESPONSIBILITY FOR ERRORS OR OMISSIONS. NEITHER IS ANY LIABILITY ASSUMED FOR DAMAGES RESULTING FROM THE USE OF INFORMATION CONTAINED HEREIN.
ISBN 9798852512543

about us

Be introduced to the two wild and wonderful connoisseurs who are taking the world by storm. They love a good tipple, a catchy tune, and a tall tale - but they're not too snooty about it. Along with their discerning taste, they're not afraid to get a little rowdy. In fact, they relish the seedier side of life, just for the fun of it. And let's not forget their feline muse, the one and only Gen. Pussy Talemonger - what a name, what a cat!

Together, they have embarked on a creative journey to write a series of books that are completely random, yet linked by their irreverent humour and general disregard for propriety. They don't care about respectability or purpose - they just want to make you laugh. They've got opinions, they've got humour, and they've got a disregard for the opinions of others - especially their friends. So don't take them too seriously, and don't take yourself too seriously either...just buckle up for a wild ride.

Come and join them on this journey of whimsy and wonder, where the joy of life is celebrated with every page.

A hundred stage tales,

In haiku's soft whispers, regale,

Truth and art prevail.

West End Plays

The Mousetrap
No Man's Land
Copenhagen
The Woman in Black
Art
Arcadia
Jerusalem
The History Boys
Blithe Spirit
The Birthday Party
Equus
The Caretaker
An Inspector Calls
Private Lives
Look Back in Anger
Journey's End
The Deep Blue Sea
Abigail's Party
Betrayal
The Homecoming
Top Girls
The Norman Conquests
Amadeus
Skylight
Translations

West End Musicals

Cats
Les Misérables
The Phantom of the Opera
Jesus Christ Superstar
Evita
Miss Saigon
Oliver!
Mamma Mia!
Billy Elliot the Musical
Matilda the Musical
We Will Rock You
Joseph and the Amazing Technicolor Dreamcoat
Sunset Boulevard
Chess
Blood Brothers
Starlight Express
Half a Sixpence
The Witches of Eastwick
Bend It Like Beckham: The Musical
Made in Dagenham
Everyone's Talking About Jamie
Me and My Girl
Bugsy Malone
Billy
Mary Poppins

Broadway Plays

Death of a Salesman
A Streetcar Named Desire
The Glass Menagerie
Who's Afraid of Virginia Woolf?
Long Day's Journey into Night
The Crucible
Angels in America
The Iceman Cometh
A Raisin in the Sun
Fences
Our Town
Proof
Doubt: A Parable
The Odd Couple
The Boys in the Band
Cat on a Hot Tin Roof
Three Tall Women
Buried Child
The Normal Heart
August: Osage County
Inherit the Wind
The Heidi Chronicles
Clybourne Park
The Children's Hour
True West

Broadway Musicals

West Side Story

The Music Man

Cabaret

Chicago

A Chorus Line

Rent

Hamilton

The Book of Mormon

Hello, Dolly!

Hairspray

Wicked

Oklahoma!

Carousel

Sweeney Todd: The Demon Barber of Fleet Street

Little Shop of Horrors

Avenue Q

Dear Evan Hansen

Fiddler on the Roof

Company

Guys and Dolls

South Pacific

The Producers

Into the Woods

Fun Home

Spring Awakening

West End Plays

West End's stage alights,

In twenty-five acts it writes,

London's theatre nights.

The Mousetrap

Secrets echo loud,
In stillness, guilt is endowed,
Innocence is shroud.

Agatha Christie

No Man's Land

Drowning in stale booze,

Reality's threads come loose,

In old age, what's true?

Harold Pinter

Copenhagen

Atoms' dance retold,

In uncertainty, truths hold,

War's physics unfold.

Michael Frayn

The Woman in Black

Shadows dance, they grin,

Fear is the true spectral sin,

Death, the kindest kin.

Stephen Mallatratt
(adapted from the novel by Susan Hill)

Art

White canvas, friends clash,

In blank spaces, values flash,

Art's price, friendship's crash.

Yasmina Reza

Arcadia

Time's dance, a duet,

Love and loss, with no regret,

Past and present, met.

Tom Stoppard

Jerusalem

Old myths, modern strife,

Rooster's tales, a rustic life,

Change cuts like a knife.

Jez Butterworth

The History Boys

Boys quest for knowledge,

Truths are questioned, norms besieged–

Learning's real homage.

Alan Bennett

Blithe Spirit

Ghosts laugh at love's plight,

Death but a mere oversight,

Forever, a blight.

Noël Coward

The Birthday Party

Party turns obscure,

In banality, fear's dish–

Reality's wish.

Harold Pinter

Equus

Horse gods, boy entranced,
In therapy, norms advanced,
Sacred, profane danced.

Peter Shaffer

The Caretaker

Trust in disrepair,

In three's dance, secrets laid bare—

Caretaker's cold stare.

Harold Pinter

An Inspector Calls

Inspector's stern call,

Society's shared downfall,

Guilt, a common thrall.

J.B. Priestley

Private Lives

Old love reignites,

Passion clashes in the night,

Hate and love unite.

Noël Coward

Look Back in Anger

Angry youth decry,

Post-war dreams become awry–

Rebellion's outcry.

John Osborne

Journey's End

War's trenches, hell's gate,
Heroism debates fate,
Death, the final mate.

R.C. Sherriff

The Deep Blue Sea

Drowned in love's despair,

Freedom in a gas-lit snare,

Vows can't breathe in air.

Terence Rattigan

Abigail's Party

Suburbia's dance,
Bitter drinks and lost romance,
Illusions enhance.

Mike Leigh

Betrayal

Love's timeline reversed,

In deceit, hearts are immersed,

Trust, forever cursed.

Harold Pinter

The Homecoming

Home's an ugly feast,
Woman's power is increased,
Love is but a beast.

Harold Pinter

Top Girls

Success at what cost,

Sisters' bonds forever lost,

In time's frost, we're tossed.

Caryl Churchill

The Norman Conquests

Love's farcical game,

Norman's conquests, who's to blame?

Passion, a wild flame.

Alan Ayckbourn

Amadeus

Genius, envy,

In music's divine frenzy,

Lies man's tragedy.

Peter Shaffer

Skylight

Past's glow, a cold light,

Love's echoes, a quiet night,

Hope is out of sight.

David Hare

Translations

Names map out a tale,

Lost in translation, words fail,

Cultures frail, set sail.

Brian Friel

West End Musicals

Melodies unfurl,

In West End's twenty-five whirls,

Each note a tale's pearl.

Cats

Felines prance at night,

For a new life, they all fight,

In song's magic light.

Andrew Lloyd Webber
T.S. Eliot, Trevor Nunn, Richard Stilgoe

Les Misérables

Justice, love collide,

In revolution's harsh tide–

Redemption's long ride.

Claude-Michel Schönberg
Herbert Kretzmer, Alain Boublil, Jean-Marc Natel, Victor Hugo

The Phantom of the Opera

Masked love sings, unseen,

In shadows of velvet sheen,

Yearning's poignant scene.

Andrew Lloyd Webber
Charles Hart, Richard Stilgoe

Jesus Christ Superstar

A star's holy plight,

Salvation in the spotlight,

It's faith or stage fright?

Andrew Lloyd Webber
Tim Rice

Evita

Evita shines bright,

Power's allure stirs the night –

A star's fickle flight.

Andrew Lloyd Webber
Tim Rice

Miss Saigon

Love in war's debris,

Saigon dreams, a tragedy,

Who is truly free?.

Claude-Michel Schönberg
Richard Maltby Jr., Alain Boublil

Oliver

An orphan's lament,

Hunger begs, who is content?

Love or a torment?

Lionel Bart
Charles Dickens

Mamma Mia

Love's old melody,

Daughter is a mystery,

What is family?

Benny Andersson, Björn Ulvaeus, Stig Anderson
Catherine Johnson

Billy Elliot the Musical

In coal dust, a dream,

Dance leaps past life's rigid scheme–

Grace in harsh light gleam.

Elton John
Lee Hall

Matilda the Musical

Girl fights with her mind,

Knowledge is a secret find,

Can truth be unkind?

Tim Minchin
Dennis Kelly, Roald Dahl

We Will Rock You

Rock rebels the norm,

In music, the spirits form,

Is silence a storm?

Queen
Ben Elton

Joseph and the Amazing Technicolor Dreamcoat

A coat's vibrant hue,

Dreams betrayed, but faith holds true,

Power subverts you.

Andrew Lloyd Webber
Tim Rice

Sunset Boulevard

Faded star's demand,
In illusions, truths remand –
Hollywood's quicksand.

Andrew Lloyd Webber
Don Black, Christopher Hampton, Billy Wilder

Chess

Game mimics the world,

In love and war, pawns are swirled–

Victories unfurled.

Benny Andersson, Björn Ulvaeus
Tim Rice, Richard Nelson

Blood Brothers

Twins part at birth's door,
Class divides, fate keeps the score–
Blood bond can't ignore.

Willy Russell

Starlight Express

Trains race through the night,

Wheels of fate spin with delight,

Dreams clash, sparks ignite.

Andrew Lloyd Webber
Richard Stilgoe, Lauren Aquilina, Don Black, Nick Coler,
David Yazbek

Half A Sixpence

Riches won and lost,

Class and love is complex cost,

Pride, the highest frost.

David Heneker, George Stiles, Anthony Drewe
Beverley Cross, Julian Fellowes

The Witches of Eastwick

Witches weave their spells,

Power seduces, then quells,

Freedom rings or knells?

Dana P. Rowe
John Dempsey

Bend It Like Beckham: The Musical

Football dreams take flight,

Tradition battles new light,

Goals beyond just white.

Howard Goodall
Charles Hart, Gurinder Chadha, Paul Mayeda Berges

Made in Dagenham

Women claim their worth,

Equality is rebirth,

What's wage's true girth?

David Arnold
Richard Bean, William Ivory

Everyone's Talking About Jamie

In heels, a boy's pride,

Prejudice is cast aside,

Who decides the stride?

Dan Gillespie Sells
Tom MacRae

Me And My Girl

Class jump, love holds tight,

Nobility redefined,

Paupers can take flight.

Noel Gay
Douglas Furber, L. Arthur Rose

Bugsy Malone

Pie fights, power's price,
Childlike mobsters roll the dice,
Innocence, our vice.

Paul Williams
Alan Parker

Billy

Liar's tales take flight,

Dreams and reality fight,

Truth unveiled at night.

John Barry
Don Black, Dick Clement, Ian La Frenais

Mary Poppins

Nanny, sky-borne wisp,

More than meets the common eye,

Chaos in her grip.

Richard M. Sherman, Robert B. Sherman,
George Stiles, Anthony Drewe, Julian Fellowes

Broadway Plays

Broadway's tales take wing,

In twenty-five dramas sing,

New York's offering.

Death of a Salesman

Dreams crumble like ash,

Salesman's tragedy takes hold,

Illusions unfold.

Arthur Miller

A Streetcar Named Desire

Desire's flaming heat,

Fading dreams on streetcar's beat,

Madness finds retreat.

Tennessee Williams

The Glass Menagerie

Fragile dreams encased,
Gentle whispers of the past,
Memories hold fast.

Tennessee Williams

Who's Afraid of Virginia Woolf?

Marital war waged,

Illusions and truths engaged,

Love's cage unassuaged.

Edward Albee

Long Day's Journey into Night

Family's haunting plight,

Darkness descends, truth takes flight,

Addiction's raw bite.

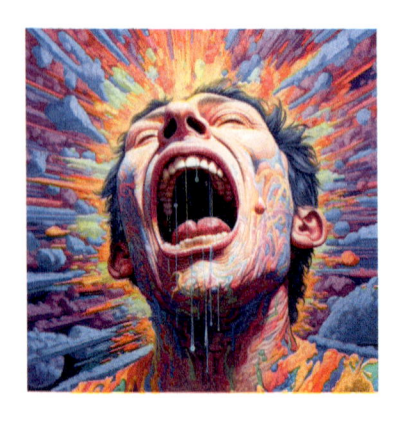

Eugene O'Neill

The Crucible

Witch-hunt's fiery breath,

Innocence condemned to death,

Truth scorched by false depths.

Arthur Miller

Angels in America

Angels descend, rise,

Lives entwined, while hope defies,

Change engulfs the skies.

Tony Kushner

The Iceman Cometh

Bar-room dreams unfold,

Illusions in liquor's hold,

Hope's icicle cold.

Eugene O'Neill

A Raisin in the Sun

Dreams deferred, arise,
Sun's warmth in family ties,
Hope beneath grey skies.

Lorraine Hansberry

Fences

Fences divide hearts,

Their dreams thwarted, life's false starts,

Bonds torn, love departs.

August Wilson

Our Town

Small town, life's embrace,

Love and death, time's fleeting trace,

Beauty in each place.

Thornton Wilder

Proof

Maths reveals the truth,

Proof of genius, lost youth,

Legacy's pursuit.

David Auburn

Doubt: A Parable

Shadows cast in doubt,

Faith and truth engage, devout,

Certainty fades out.

John Patrick Shanley

The Odd Couple

Mismatched friends collide,

Oddity, love cannot hide,

Laughter by their side.

Neil Simon

The Boys in the Band

Secrets in their hearts,

Masks unravel, love restarts,

Friendship's fragile arts.

Mart Crowley

Cat on a Hot Tin Roof

Lies scorch like the sun,

Desire's battle, wounds won,

Masks melt one by one.

Tennessee Williams

Three Tall Women

Three lives intertwined,

Time's passage, memories bind,

Aging's bitter rind.

Edward Albee

Buried Child

Family's buried sins,

Secrets, shame, darkness begins,

Truth's redemption spins.

Sam Shepard

The Normal Heart

Love battles disease,

Activism finds its ease,

Hearts scream for release.

Larry Kramer

August: Osage County

Family's stormy strife,

Secrets carve a painful life,

Dysfunction runs rife.

Tracy Letts

Inherit the Wind

Science clashes faith,

In the courtroom's heated wraith,

Truth's fire shall bathe.

Jerome Lawrence
Robert Edwin Lee

The Heidi Chronicles

Feminism's face,

Heidi's journey finds its place,

Identity's chase.

Wendy Wasserstein

Clybourne Park

Shifting times reveal,

Secrets buried, tensions steal,

Housing's wounds unheal.

Bruce Norris

The Children's Hour

Whispers taint pure hearts,
Children's lies tear lives apart,
Truth's burden imparts.

Lillian Hellman

True West

Brothers' rivalry,

Desert's heat, reality,

Identity's plea.

Sam Shepard

Broadway Musicals

Broadway tunes resound,

Twenty-five musicals bound,

New York's heartbeat found.

West Side Story

Dance on concrete, war.

Love found, just to be lost, strange,

Dream of peace, guns roar.

Leonard Bernstein
Stephen Sondheim, Arthur Laurents

The Music Man

Music healed a town,
Scam turned truth, a twist of fate,
In deceit, love found.

Meredith Willson

Cabaret

Dark, dance-filled Berlin,

The world's a stage, masking pain,

Freedom's fleeting sin.

John Kander
Fred Ebb, Joe Masteroff

Chicago

Fame through blood, a jest,

Notoriety, the best,

Justice? A mere guest.

John Kander
Fred Ebb, Bob Fosse

A Chorus Line

Dreams born in the line,

Success costs a soul, sometimes.

Dance, and let it shine.

Marvin Hamlisch
Edward Kleban, James Kirkwood Jr., Nicholas Dante

Rent

Life in arrears owed,

Can love pay the debt we hold?

Hearts can't be foreclosed.

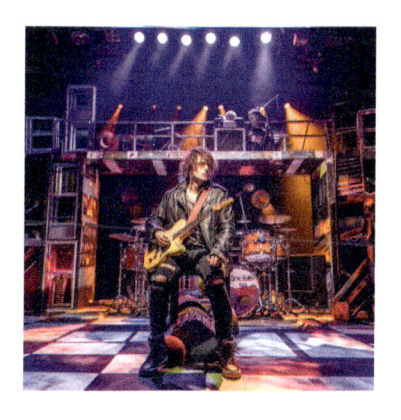

Jonathan Larson

Hamilton

Founding Father, bright,

An immigrant's fight is might,

History rewrites.

Lin-Manuel Miranda

The Book of Mormon

Missionaries' quest,

Faith and satire intertwine,

Laughs, lessons infest.

Trey Parker,
Robert Lopez, Matt Stone

Hello, Dolly!

Matchmaking delight,

Dolly's charm shines ever bright,

Love finds its true height.

Jerry Herman
Michael Stewart

Hairspray

Dancing 'round the beat,

Inclusion's rhythm takes seat,

Love's power, pure, sweet.

Marc Shaiman
Scott Wittman, Mark O'Donnell, Thomas Meehan

Wicked

Emerald-skinned outcast,

Friendship defies wicked past,

Gravity is cast.

Stephen Schwartz
Winnie Holzman

Oklahoma!

Prairie dreams take flight,

Love and hope, in golden light,

Oklahoma's might.

Richard Rodgers
Oscar Hammerstein II

Carousel

Round, round life's cruel ride,

A villain's love, cannot hide,

Redemption's low tide.

Richard Rodgers
Oscar Hammerstein II

Sweeney Todd:
The Demon Barber of Fleet Street

Revenge served hot and neat,

On pie plates, a bitter treat,

Justice can be sweet.

Stephen Sondheim
Hugh Wheeler

Little Shop of Horrors

Man-eating plant thrives,

Greedy desires take lives,

Beware, dark demise.

Alan Menken
Howard Ashman

Avenue Q

Puppets learn of strife,

Adulting's not black and white–

Strings of real life, rife.

Robert Lopez, Jeff Marx
Jeff Whitty

Dear Evan Hansen

Lonely heart finds voice,
In lies, connection's false choice,
Truth brings healing's poise.

Benj Pasek, Justin Paul
Steven Levenson

Fiddler on the Roof

Tradition's old song,

In change, where do we belong?

The roof, weak yet strong.

Jerry Bock
Sheldon Harnick, Joseph Stein

Company

Love's company, rare,

Alone in crowds, common scare,

Connection, life's dare.

Stephen Sondheim
George Furth

Guys and Dolls

Gamblers, love bets stowed,

Virtue meets vice at crossroad–

Dice cast, hearts bestowed.

Frank Loesser
Jo Swerling, Abe Burrows

South Pacific

War-torn lover's song,

Prejudice, a lifelong wrong,

Love, where we belong.

Richard Rodgers
Oscar Hammerstein II

The Producers

Showbiz's wild ride,

Two schemers seek fame's high tide,

Laughs bloom nationwide.

Mel Brooks
Thomas Meehan

Into the Woods

Fairy tales unwound,

In the woods, ourselves we found,

Life's merry-go-round.

Stephen Sondheim
James Lapine

Fun Home

Family's hidden pain,

Memories, truths intertwine,

Finding self, refrain.

Jeanine Tesori
Lisa Kron

Spring Awakening

Youth in quiet strife,

Blossoming to harsh life's rife—

Awake, cut like knife.

Duncan Sheik
Steven Sater

If you enjoyed this, read more in the series:

"The Haiku Stage: Dramatic Verses, Operatic Curses!"

A captivating series of books that ingeniously encapsulates the plots of operas, plays, and musicals using the elegance of haikus. Each book unveils a collection of haikus, carefully crafted to capture the essence of well-known theatrical works. Dive into a world where concise poetry meets the power of storytelling, as these haikus transport you into the heart of each performance.

With brevity and artistry, "The Haiku Stage: Dramatic Verses, Operatic Curses!" celebrates the rich tapestry of the performing arts, offering a unique and memorable way to experience beloved works of theatre.

Printed in Great Britain
by Amazon